Bitch
Bitch
Bitch

'BITCH! BITCH! BITCH!' is a unique collection of some of the more vindictive remarks made around the entertainment business in recent years. It is NOT intended to upset, offend, or add insult to injury, but . . .

The Authors, 1990

David Wheeler and Mike Wrenn

A DELL TRADE PAPERBACK

A DELL TRADE PAPERBACK
Published by Dell Publishing, a division of Bantam Doubleday Dell Publishing
Group, Inc.
666 Fifth Avenue
New York, New York 10103

This book is a revised edition and was previously published in Great Britain by Omnibus
Press.

ISBN: 0-440-50310-8

All photographs supplied by London Features International, Pictorial Press, and Starfile
Art Direction by Mike Bell
Book Design by Giant
Photo Research by Paul Giblin
Goddess: Margaux Ravis

Packaged by Rapid Transcript, a division of March Tenth, Inc.

Printed in the United States of America
Published simultaneously in Canada
10 9 8 7 6 5 4 3 2 1
RRH

Illegitimus non carborundum*

There ain't nothing new in this business. Stealing is a grand and glorious tradition ir television, and I'm proud to be a part of it.

Pat Sajak, on Arsenio Hall's calling him a "Carson clone," 1989

Good heavens, television is something you appear on; you don't watch.
Noel Coward

I hate television. I hate it as much as peanuts. But I can't stop eating peanuts.
Orson Welles, 1956

TV—chewing gum for the eyes.
Frank Lloyd Wright

The ultimate game show will be one where somebody gets killed at the end.
Chuck Barris

Television has proved that people will look at anything rather than each other.
Ann Landers

It is a medium of entertainment which permits millions of people to listen to the same joke at the same time, and yet remain lonesome.
T. S. Eliot, on television, 1963

I spent all my time trying to bring lousy scripts . . . [and] mannequins with suits on to life.
Robert Blake, on his show "Baretta"

When I lie in the sack and flick on the remote switch and look at the box, I see things like "Let's Make A Deal"—a clinical study in avarice and greed where perspiring yo-yos go into convulsions trying to latch onto a warehouse full of free acquisitions while the studio audience screams and gurgles.

I see "The Dating Game," where a vapid, mini-skirted beauty throws out well-rehearsed, thinly veiled sexual asides to a trio who are obviously lusting for her body.

I see the dregs of television, "Gilligan's Island" and "Hee Haw," and all the havoc and damage that man can wreak on his fellow man.
Rod Serling, 1973

An actor wouldn't wipe his ass with any page from any one of the scripts we'd done . . . we were always pointing guns at people, always saying, "What are you doing on the Ponderosa?" Well, my attitude was, Who the hell *cares?* Let 'em be there!
Lorne Greene, on "Bonanza," 1960

A hyena in syrup.
Yevgeny Yevtushenko, on Barbara Walters

I was going to have a mob of centenarians find Bryant and gum him to death.
NBC weatherman Willard Scott, on his feud with colleague Bryant Gumbel, 1989

Look at Morton Downey's show. Nothing but louts! Wall-to-wall louts! It's frightening!

Norman Mailer, 1989

The one function that TV news performs very well is that when there is no news we give it to you with the same emphasis as if there were news.

David Brinkley

His sense of humor is horseshit and I feel sorry for him.

Bryant Gumbel, on David Letterman

He does not speak as much as exhale, and he exhales polysyllabically.

Edwin Newman, on William F. Buckley, Jr.

Like, I can't be on none of those television shows, 'cause I'd have to tell Johnny Carson, "You're a sad motherfucker." That's the only way I could put it.

Miles Davis

I've sort of been doing the talk show in my head for thirty years. I played talk show as a kid. My poor brothers would have to watch me interview myself. I was a sick, sick human being.

Pat Sajak, 1989

The yuppie is even thinner and sillier than the yippie. The yippie was bad enough. The yippie was less interesting than the hippie, and the hippie, in his turn, had less of a mind than the bohemian. We're developing a society that I would call a lout society.

When I die they'll bury me three feet down. I am very shallow.

Joan Rivers

Does this mean I don't have to do "The Merv Griffin Show"?

Peter Frampton, following his near fatal car crash, 1978

The only thing that could fuck it up now is what fucks up everything—success.

Lorne Michaels, producer of "Saturday Night Live"

[Like] a black widow. Screw 'em and eat 'em.

Victoria Principal, on how to treat producers and be successful in television

While the appeal of "The Patty Duke Show" is not hard to understand, I still don't have a handle on the success of the six albums I made for United Artists. . . . Even the covers still give me a pain in the stomach. I look like a forty-year-old pygmy on one, on another I have white hair with black roots, like an early punker, well ahead of my time.

Patty Duke

A hymn to overstatement if there ever was one.

Mr. Blackwell, on Joan Collins, 1989

Mall fashion at its worst.

Mr. Blackwell, on Vanna White, 1989

A football player in drag.

Mr. Blackwell, on Kim Novak, 1990

Takes thrift-shop chic to the terrifying limit.

Mr. Blackwell, on Roseanne Barr, 1989

His head looks like my crotch.

Roseanne Barr, on Arsenio Hall

Trianglehead.

Roseanne Barr, on Arsenio Hall

The only reason I'm in Hollywood is that I don't have the moral courage to refuse the money.

Marlon Brando

Film people are so fucking arrogant. I hate them.

Elton John

The governors of the music branch of the Academy are assholes.

Robert Stigwood, manager of the Bee Gees

Slime, just barely passing for human beings.

Steven Soderbergh, director of *Sex, Lies & Videotape,* on producers, 1989

Nothing would disgust me more, morally, than receiving an Oscar.

Luis Bunuel, 1971

They come for you in the morning in a limousine; they take you to the studio; they stick a pretty girl in your arms . . . They call that a profession? Come on!

Marcello Mastroianni

A face that convinces you that God is a cartoonist.

Jack Kroll, movie critic, on Woody Allen

One of my unfavorite directors, if I may say so, is [Michelangelo] Antonioni, because he tells the same story all the time in the same style. To me he is like a fly that tries to go out of a window and doesn't realize there is glass, and keeps banging against it, and never reaches the sky.

Franco Zefferelli

It seems that boredom is one of the great discoveries of our time. If so, there's no question but that he must be considered a pioneer.

Luchino Visconti, director, on fellow director Michelangelo Antonioni

I hate my films, and I do not wish to talk about them.

Michelangelo Antonioni

Robotic, the way he handles people.

Eddie Murphy, on Dan Aykroyd

I'm *infinitely* better-looking than Arsenio. He has huge gums and these long, fucked-up fingers. Course, he's always telling me I'm fucking ugly.

Eddie Murphy, on Arsenio Hall, 1990

You bastard . . . you cheat . . . you drunken bum . . . I got enough on you to hang you. By the time I get through with you you'll be as broke as when you got here. You goddamn spic . . . you . . . you wetback!

Lucille Ball to Desi Arnaz, upon his saying he couldn't live with her anymore

She was a little tight with a buck. At her daughter's first wedding, out by the pool, catered, it was almost like a "Lucy" sketch. She'd just sold Desilu studios [for $17 million] but she had cold cuts and paper plates. She had no knowledge of the correct, chic thing to do.

Jack Carter, on Lucille Ball

I regret the passing of the studio system. I was very appreciative of it because I had no talent. Believe me. What could I do? I couldn't dance. I couldn't sing. I could *talk.* I could barely walk. I had no flair. I wasn't a beauty, that's for sure.

Lucille Ball

All I can say is that when I'm trying to play serious love scenes with her, she's positioning her bottom for the best angle shots.

Actor Stephen Boyd, on Brigitte Bardot

Anyone who has come close to Warren [Beatty] has shed quite a few feathers. He tends to maul you.

Leslie Caron

Every time I go on a talk show, I am invariably asked about Warren Beatty's sex life. I have a stock answer: "He should be in a jar at the Harvard Medical School."

Rex Reed

I never took him seriously. . . . A lot of women like somebody who's that smooth. In the beginning Warren was pretty good pretending he was only smooth on the outside and a bowl of jelly on the inside. But he doesn't do that secondary act very well now.

Carly Simon, on Warren Beatty, 1989

Sex is the most important thing in his life.

**Shirley Maclaine, on her
brother, Warren Beatty**

Ms. Bergen has displayed the same emotional range and dramatic intensity as her father's dummy, Charlie McCarthy.

**Film critics Harry and Michael
Medved, on Candice Bergen's
acting ability**

I just don't know what the hell he's after.

**Frank Capra, on Ingmar
Bergman**

[I] hated that bastard.

**William Holden, on Humphrey
Bogart**

Bogart's a helluva nice guy till eleven-thirty P.M. After that he thinks he's Bogart.

**Dave Chasen of Chasen's
restaurant in Los Angeles**

Peter Bogdanovich wanted to do it [*The Long Goodbye*] with Robert Mitchum or Lee Marvin. The way he does all his films—as photostats of other films.

Robert Altman

Actors like him are good, but on the whole I do not enjoy actors who seek to commune with their armpits, so to speak.

Greer Garson, on Marlon Brando

Montgomery Clift was an exceptionally bright man who liked to pretend he wasn't, unlike Brando, who likes to pretend he's bright whereas in fact he isn't really.

Edward Dmytryk, director

The greatest screen actor in the history of cinema—perhaps—and he's running around with white hair and a Krypton suit. Just something wrong about that.

**James Woods, on Marlon
Brando's appearance in
*Superman***

I want to be the girl in *Indiana Jones.* I would love to do an adventure movie where I was saving the world. It might be cool if I used a lot of kitchen tools to fight off the enemy.

Roseanne Barr

She's common, she can't act—yet she's the hottest female property around these days. If that doesn't tell you something about the state of our industry today, what does?

Stewart Granger, on Joan Collins, 1984

Whatever Francis [Ford Coppola] does for you always ends up benefitting Francis the most.

George Lucas

Coppola couldn't piss in a pot.

Bob Hoskins

There is not enough money in Hollywood to lure me into making another picture with Joan Crawford. And I like money.

Sterling Hayden

I wouldn't give you one dime for those two washed-up bitches.

Jack Warner, to Bob Aldrich, director of *Whatever Happened to Baby Jane?*, on Bette Davis and Joan Crawford

That bitch is loaded half the time.

Bette Davis, on Joan Crawford

Acting has absolutely nothing to do with anything important.

Marlon Brando

Mooning: A quaint custom popularized by Marlon Brando.

Jim Backus

He's like all these drunks. Impossible when he's drunk and only half there when he's sober. Wooden as a board with his body, relies on doing all his acting with his voice.

John Boorman, on Richard Burton, 1984

Andy Warhol in a cassock.

Film critic Robert Hughes, on Richard Chamberlain in *The Thorn Birds*

I said that I didn't think Chevy Chase could ad-lib a fart after a baked-bean dinner. I think he took umbrage at that a little bit.

Johnny Carson

Toward the end of her life, she [Joan Crawford] looked like a hungry insect magnified a million times—a praying mantis that had forgotten how to pray.

Quentin Crisp, 1989

I don't really like people much. I mean, I know I should like develop this passion for other people and like get to know them, but I couldn't care less.

Sandy Dennis, on her relationship with Liz Taylor and Richard Burton during the filming of *Who's Afraid of Virginia Woolf*

Pauline Kael has aptly observed that Miss [Sandy] Dennis "has made an acting style out of postnasal drip." It should be added that she balanced her postnasal condition with something like prefrontal lobotomy, so that when she is not a walking catarrh she is a blithering imbecile.

John Simon, 1968

Christ! You never know what size boobs that broad has strapped on! She must have a different set for each day of the week! She's supposed to be shriveling away, but her tits keep growing. I keep running into them like Hollywood Hills.

Bette Davis, on Joan Crawford

The best time I ever had with Joan Crawford was when I pushed her down the stairs in *Whatever Happened to Baby Jane?*

Bette Davis

The only real talent Miss Day possesses is that of being absolutely sanitary: Her personality untouched by human emotions, her brow unclouded by human thought, her form unsmudged by the slightest evidence of femininity . . . this spun-sugar zombie. . . ."

John Simon, on Doris Day, 1967

I don't mean to speak ill of the dead, but he was a prick—pardon my French. He was selfish and petulant, and believed his own press releases. On the set, he'd upstage an actor and step on his lines. Arrogant.

Rock Hudson, on James Dean

Dean *was* a cripple anyway, inside— he was not like Brando. People compared them, but there was no similarity. He was a far, far sicker kid, and Brando's not sick, he's just troubled.

Elia Kazan

I shared drugs with my dad many times when I was in my twenties. We had no relationship, really.

Jamie Lee Curtis, on her father, Tony Curtis, 1989

. . . a Class-A bastard.

Liza Minnelli, on Robert DeNiro

I can never recognize him from one movie to the next, so I never know who he is. To me he's just an invisible man. He doesn't exist.

Truman Capote, on Robert DeNiro

Next to Will Durant, no. Next to Victoria Principal, brilliant. Victoria Principal has to read a thousand books to become low-brow.

Joan Rivers, when asked if Bo Derek is bright, 1984

. . . underneath there's just a little boy saying, "Can I just have my mommy?"

Laura Dern, on her father, Bruce Dern, 1986

There is a whole group of people in America who do nothing but sit around in dark rooms in the Museum of Modern Art and watch old movies. Don't they have anything more important to do with their lives?

Marlene Dietrich

The first time I saw it was on a press junket. There was supposed to be a party after the film. I went back to my cabin, took two Seconals and a slug of Scotch. . . . It was a very embarrassing thing.

Jacqueline Susann, on the film adaptation of *Valley of the Dolls*

. . . I need an air-sick bag to sit through that movie.

Patty Duke, on her role in *Valley of the Dolls*

Keir Dullea and gone tomorrow.

Noel Coward

She was a gigantic pain in the ass. She demonstrated certifiable proof of insanity.

Roman Polanski, on Faye Dunaway

He isn't an actor, so one could hardly call him a bad actor. He'd have to do something before we could consider him bad at it.

Pauline Kael, on Clint Eastwood

That was just the style of the times. People liked to throw around the term "fascist." It didn't bother me, because I knew she was full of shit the whole time.

Clint Eastwood, on Pauline Kael's pan of *Dirty Harry*

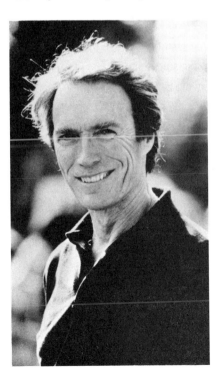

A man of many talents, all of them minor.

Critic Leslie Halliwell, on Blake Edwards

The reason I drink is because when I'm sober I think I'm Eddie Fisher.

Dean Martin

And Peter [Fonda] couldn't act. I'm sorry, man, he just can't act. He never bothered to sit and learn. He never studied. And he just kind of larked out. Now I don't begrudge the fact that he has talent. But he's not an actor, by any stretch of the imagination.

Bruce Dern

And then there's also the possibility of doing something with my sister. Listen, Jane and me in a film, right? Directed by [Roger] Vadim, right? Who's got one of the greatest love cameras I've ever seen, a *phallus!* Jane and I as brother and sister who make nude pornographic movies directed by her husband, who is a porny moviemaker, and our old man is a has-been actor who's drunk all the time. Everybody would go see it.

Peter Fonda, c. 1968

He was a sadist.

John Carradine, on John Ford

Zsa Zsa! Go *home* to your dogs!

Tom Snyder, on Zsa Zsa Gabor

She was landed with an idiot giggle, a remorseless inclination to squeak, and if a brain hummed behind those dumbfounded eyes, the secret never leaked out.

Donald Zec, columnist, on Goldie Hawn

You're born, you live, you get some terrible disease and get knocked off. I think it's a relief to be alive—if you can enjoy life. And it's a relief to be dead, if you enjoy sleeping.

Katharine Hepburn, 1989

He was macabre. When I was a little girl he sent me a gift of a replica of my mother, Tippi Hedren, in a coffin. That was his idea of a joke. He had a sick sense of humor. After that, Mother never worked for him again.

Melanie Griffith, on Alfred Hitchcock

I wish somebody would come out and say the lady has Parkinson's Disease. Because my joke is: Nobody told me. I threw out two perfectly good TV sets. I thought something was the matter with the set.

Joan Rivers, on Katharine Hepburn

This much idiot no one has ever been in the world!

Klaus Kinski, on Werner Herzog, 1989

He's not aging well. The best thing to happen to his career is for him to die immediately.

Werner Herzog, on Klaus Kinski

It seems to me that the world is rapidly becoming a very peculiar place. There's no discipline left. Sad. But people are glutted with desire and then they need the psychiatrist. Well, for $80 an hour, you better kill yourself.

Katharine Hepburn, 1989

The trouble with him is he doesn't think he's just a hired actor, like the rest of us. He thinks he's the *entire* production.

Richard Harris, on Charlton Heston

He's done the hippie thing, and the *Easy Rider* thing, and the gross thing. . . . And he really does have this evil twin side to him. You know, that "Come on, mannnn!" thing. But in fact, he's Mr. Armani suits, and abstract paintings, and he's got this Frank Gehry–designed house. He's a fifty-three-year-old man who wears bifocals!

Jodie Foster, on Dennis Hopper, 1989

I don't understand this Method stuff. I remember Laurence Olivier asking Dustin Hoffman why he stayed up all night. Dustin, looking really beat, really bad, said it was to get into the scene being filmed that day in which he was supposed to have been up all night. Olivier said, "My boy, if you'd learn how to act you wouldn't have to stay up all night."

Robert Mitchum

Daryl Hannah remains a rotten actress and still looks like a linebacker in a Lorelei wig.

John Simon

Richard can't help it if he's known in the business as "the horizontal champ," can he? When it comes to doing anything dangerous on the set, he's usually found flat on his back. I'm a far better cowboy than he is. But then, to be fair, I'm a younger man. And I'm prettier. And I have more hair than he has.

Oliver Reed, on Richard Harris

A testicle with legs.

Pauline Kael, on Bob Hoskins

I hired William Hurt for *Altered States,* and found I was his analyst for six months. . . .

Ken Russell, 1987

I've seen him turn into this arrogant, sour, ceremonial, piously chauvinistic egomaniac.

Elliot Gould, on Jerry Lewis

A series of visual explosions that hurt my ears and gave me a headache. I couldn't watch. I don't really consider that direction.

Joseph Mankiewicz, on George Lucas and Stephen Spielberg's Indiana Jones movies, 1989

Well, I did go out with him a few times; in fact, a few of the Go-Go's went out with him. We passed him around.

Belinda Carlisle, on Rob Lowe, 1989

I was actually forever grateful when she won [the Oscar] because I thought that would shut her up for a while. Imagine my dismay when she just kept having fiftieth birthdays and doing interviews. Jack Nicholson called me up for her second fiftieth and said, "Didn't we celebrate her fiftieth birthday in Texas?"

Debra Winger, on Shirley Maclaine

A Steve McQueen performance just naturally lends itself to monotony: Steve doesn't bring much to the party.

Robert Mitchum

. . . her oars aren't touching the water these days.

Dean Martin, on Shirley Maclaine

Everyone's just laughing at me. I hate it. Big breasts, big ass, big deal. Can't I be anything else?

Marilyn Monroe

It's better for the whole world to know you, even as a sex star, than never to be known at all.
Marilyn Monroe

Directing her was like directing Lassie.
Otto Preminger, on Marilyn Monroe

It's like kissing Hitler.
Tony Curtis, on Marilyn Monroe

Marilyn? Surely you are referring to Hollywood's Joan of Arc, aren't you? The Legend? Our Ultimate Sacrificial Lamb? She was the meanest woman I have ever met around this town. I am appalled by this cult. It's getting to be an act of courage to say anything but saintly things about her . . . I have never met anyone as utterly mean as Marilyn Monroe.
Billy Wilder

I have just come from the Actor's Studio, where I saw Marilyn Monroe. . . . She had no girdle on, her ass was hanging out. She is a disgrace to the industry.
Joan Crawford

A vacuum with nipples.
Otto Preminger, on Marilyn Monroe

She was good at playing abstract confusion in the same way a dwarf is good at being short.
Clive James, on Marilyn Monroe

Dramatic art in her opinion is knowing how to fill a sweater.
Bette Davis, on Jayne Mansfield

He looked at me like he had just smelled a pile of dead fish. Like I was a leper, or something awful. He'd say something like, ''Oh how simply ravishing, my dear.'' But he really wanted to throw up.
Marilyn Monroe, on Sir Laurence Olivier

I am a limited actor. My range isn't that great and I don't have that much scope.
Steve McQueen

One thing about Steve, he didn't like the women in his life to have balls.
Ali McGraw, on Steve McQueen

I'd let my wife, children, and animals starve before I'd subject myself to something like that again.
Director Don Siegel, on working with Bette Midler, 1989

You always come out sounding like one of those jerks in *Interview*.

Andrew McCarthy, on avoiding interviews, 1988

I always thought Miss Minnelli's face deserving—of first prize in the beagle category. . . . It is a face going off in three directions simultaneously: the nose always en route to becoming a trunk, blubber lips unable to resist the pull of gravity, and a chin trying its damnedest to withdraw into the neck. . . .

John Simon, on Liza Minnelli

[In the future], he has a better chance of working with Vic Morrow than with me.

Eddie Murphy, on *Coming to America* director John Landis

His life is cars and girls, girls and cars. More cars. More girls.

Jamie Lee Curtis, on Eddie Murphy

[A] Hollywood Negro.

Spike Lee, on Eddie Murphy, 1989

Eddie can hear the rustle of nylon stockings at fifty yards.

Director Walter Hill, on Eddie Murphy

Nichols' work is frivolous—charming, light, and titanically inconsequential. . . . What Nichols is is brilliant. Brilliant and trivial and self-serving and frigid.

William Goldman, on Mike Nichols

I'll do it if I can play him as a schizophrenic.

Nick Nolte, when offered the title part in *Superman*

She left a kitten at the airport when she was little. I just know she's going to do the same thing with the baby.

Ryan O'Neal, on his daughter Tatum O'Neal's childbirth

CITY OF WESTMINSTER

If you had been any prettier, it would have been Florence of Arabia.
Noel Coward, to Peter O'Toole

Pacino is a schmuck.
Oliver Stone, on Al Pacino

Did we get along? We never really, uh, talked—I think by Sean's design.
Michael J. Fox, on Sean Penn

What I figure is that if you're an actor and your career is in a bit of a lull because you just broke up with someone more famous than you and you need to get your photo in a newspaper, wouldn't you want to go and hang out with a trendy band?
Michelle Shocked, on why Sean Penn was hanging out with her opening band, The Cowboy Junkies, 1989

It's hard to drink as much bourbon as I do and be an actor.
George Peppard

Don't anybody criticize me because I was in a lot of crap! Sometimes you're lucky to even get crap!
George Peppard

He's really Martin Bormann in elevator shoes, with a face-lift by a blindfolded plastic surgeon in Luxembourg.
Billy Wilder, on Otto Preminger

Otto Preminger is only happy if everybody else is miserable.
Michael Caine

Can you imagine the pride a man like Laurence Olivier has to swallow to make a movie for a man like Otto Preminger?
Actress Shirley Knight

I'm not a member of a swinging set. I hate Gilbert & Sullivan and boys with long hair and discotheques.
Lynn Redgrave

[Robert] Redford is a dangerous man to let loose on the streets. He has holes in his head, he should be arrested.
George Roy Hill

When I worked on *The Seven Percent Solution*, Vanessa Redgrave tried to convert me to a form of communism, Trotskyism, whatever the hell it is. Talented broad, but everyone ducked behind a camera when she came around. I asked her, ''Vanessa, can you shoot a pistol?'' ''Why?'' ''Well, when the revolution comes . . .'' ''No, no,'' she interrupted. ''Someone else will do that.'' Some Trotskyite. She travels by Rolls-Royce.

Robert Duvall

Do you know what I am? I'm successful. Destroy me and you destroy your British film industry. Keep me going and I'm the biggest star you've got. I'm Mr. England.

Oliver Reed

Don't you know what they're doing is fucking posters of Redford in the alleys of Rome? You don't have to worry about acting. All you need is to get a poster they can fuck in the alleys of Rome.

Raquel Welch

An arrogant, self-centered, petulant individual. I don't say this in any demeaning way.

Bob Guccione, on Ken Russell

Maybe I can't do what Vanessa Redgrave can, but can Vanessa Redgrave do what I can do? Who's kidding who here?

Raquel Welch

I haven't seen the picture and I intend to go on not seeing the picture, so that when people ask what I think about it I can tell them I haven't seen it.

Paddy Chayevsky, after taking his name off the credits of *Altered States*

Each anecdote that he tells, each film incident he recalls, seems to be prefaced by the memory of disease. His asthma is well enough known but as his memory unfurls it becomes punctuated by "Oh yeah, I'd just got up from double pneumonia," or "that was when I had the flu," as if illness was the prerequisite rather than the neurotic result of any artistic endeavor.

Chris Peachment, film critic, on Martin Scorsese

I'm Number Ten [at the box office]. Right under Barbra Streisand. Can you imagine being under Barbra Streisand? Get me a bag, I may throw up.

Walter Matthau

. . . one of the best actors alive. But my opinion of him as an actor is much higher than my opinion of him as a man.

John Huston, on George C. Scott

Nobody here believes that there's a man alive who can control that asshole.

Producer Mike J. Frankovich, on Peter Sellers

I think his mother had gained such an incredible influence over him that he virtually abdicated his own rights to any individual personality. Finally, he had to invade other bodies to register at all. He had to inhabit; he was like a ghoul, he had to feast off somebody else! But he did it so well, it became an art. He was not a genius, Sellers, he was a freak.

Spike Milligan, comedian, on Peter Sellers

Sellers became a monster. He just got bored with the part [Inspector Clouseau] and became angry, sullen, and unprofessional. He wouldn't show up for work and he began looking for anyone to blame but himself for his own madness, his own craziness.

Blake Edwards

. . . Sinatra's behavior was unbelievable. There was an old lady playing the slot machines nearby, and this annoyed him. . . . he kicked a couple of bottles of champagne towards her and said, ''Get away, you're bothering me.'' . . . we weren't given any choice [of what to eat]. He chose wieners and sauerkraut for everyone. And there was more trouble. Sinatra decided he didn't like the pianist. So he tossed a handful of coins at him and told him to take off. That did it. My friend and I got up and left.

Valerie Perrine, on Frank Sinatra, 1974

Unpleasant man. No one has yet worked out what makes him tick.

Robert Aldrich, on Frank Sinatra

He's the kind of guy that, when he dies, he's going up to heaven and give God a bad time for making him bald.

Marlon Brando, on Frank Sinatra

I always knew Frank would end up in bed with a boy.

Ava Gardner, on ex-husband Frank Sinatra's marriage to Mia Farrow

. . . like cracking the whip at a limping horse.

Franco Zefferelli, on directing Brooke Shields in Endless Love

When Sinatra dies, they're giving his zipper to the Smithsonian.

Dean Martin

Not that he would pay me that to write a script.

Orson Wells, upon learning that Steven Spielberg had paid $50,000 for the sled Rosebud, used in Citizen Kane.

. . . Sylvester Stallone . . . I bet he has pimples on his ass.

John Waters

His big asset: a face that would look well upon a three-toed sloth. There is not much that is human about the droop of those four A.M. eyelids, and what there is recalls a man who has been either slugged or drugged into a sinister quiescence. If not the Incredible, Stallone is at least the Improbable Hulk.

Russell Davies, on Sylvester Stallone, 1977

Barbra Streisand's a *dawg*, as is Bette Midler. I mean, she's got big tits, but thank God she's got them, because she hasn't got anything else. Streisand's got long fingernails and a good voice, but her *face*! It looks as though a truck ran into it.

Divine, 1983

Oh God, she looks like a chicken.

Truman Capote, on Meryl Streep

But oh, how she suffers. In this interview she was agonizing about having to meet the press. She was moaning that she didn't want a lot of people around. And I wanted to ask her, ''Then why the hell are you an actress?'' They're so damned sincere these days.

George Cukor, on Meryl Streep, 1986

She has a double chin and an overdeveloped chest and she's rather short in the leg. So I can hardly describe her as the most beautiful creature I've ever seen.

Richard Burton, on Elizabeth Taylor, c. 1963

Is she fat? Her favorite food is seconds.

Joan Rivers, on Elizabeth Taylor

Wobbling her enormous derriere across the screen [in *Hammersmith Is Out*] in a manner so offensive it would bring litigation from any dignified, self-respecting performer; and saying lines like: "I'm the biggest mother of them all" inspires pity instead of laughs. She has been announcing plans to retire from the screen. Now is as good a time as any.

Rex Reed, on Elizabeth Taylor, 1972

[A] fat little kewpie doll.

Andy Warhol, on Elizabeth Taylor

Filming with Streisand is an experience which may have cured me of movies.

Kris Kristofferson, 1981

She's a real "kvetch". . . . But I can handle that. When she's "kvetching" I simply say: "Shut up and give me a little kiss, will you, huh?" or "Stick out your boobs, they're beautiful." And after that she's fine for the next ten minutes.

Peter Bogdanovich, on Barbra Streisand

I have never met anyone so badly behaved.

James Mason, on Raquel Welch

She's silicone from the knees up.

George Masters, on Raquel Welch

If I were on a plane and there were an earthquake and all of California fell into the sea and there were no movie actors left, if I landed and called up the studios and said, "Hey, fellas, I'm still here, there's one left," some executive would say, "Well, yeah, but I'm sure there's a football player in Kansas who would be better for the part. Just stay at the airport. We'll get back to you."

James Woods, 1989

Perhaps the most hostile of all American actors.

Pauline Kael, on James Woods

Does the word "nightmare" mean anything to you?

James Woods, on his relationship with Sean Young

I go to the park sick as a dog, and wher I see my uniform hanging there, I get well right away.

Then I see some of you guys, and I get sick again.

It was a brain transplant. I got a sportswriter's brain so I could be sure I had one that hadn't been used.

Norm Van Brocklin, former NFL quarterback and coach, when asked about his brain surgery two years earlier, 1981

All pro athletes are bilingual. They speak English and profanity.

Gordie Howe

Most guys who write about sports are just little overweight creeps.

Pete Maravich

I like the people, the talk, even the dinners, I love everything about hockey except the games.

Glenn Hall, St. Louis Blues goaltender

If it's pretty skating they want, let 'em go to the Ice Capades.

Fred Shero, Philadelphia Flyers coach, on criticism of his team's "on-rink style"

I went to a fight the other night and a hockey game broke out.

Rodney Dangerfield, 1978

Forecheck, backcheck, paycheck.

Gil Perreault, Buffalo Sabres center, on the primary elements of hockey

Sometimes I wish I was a dog and Howard was a tree.

Muhammad Ali, on Howard Cosell

Not while I'm alive.

Irving Rudd, boxing publicist, on Howard Cosell's statement that he was his own worst enemy, 1986

After the fight is over and Frazier don't answer the bell, I'm gonna jump over the ropes and I'm gonna whup Howard Cosell.

Muhammad Ali

I'd go ten more rounds with Holmes if I thought it would get Cosell off football broadcasts.

Tex Cobb, whose loss to Larry Holmes in 1982 prompted Howard Cosell to quit boxing telecasts, 1983

Fighters are just brutes who come to entertain the rich white people. The masters get two of us big buck slaves and let us fight it out while they bet, "My slave can whip your slave."

Cassius Clay (Muhammad Ali), 1964

Who would pay a nickel for another Patterson-Liston fight? I know I wouldn't.

Floyd Patterson, on the possibility of a rematch with Sonny Liston, 1964

I am a coward. . . . My fighting has little to do with that fact, though. I mean you can be a fighter—and a *winning* fighter—and still be a coward.

Floyd Patterson, 1964

[Muhammad Ali] is a pelvic missionary. He's laid more ugly women than you'd ever believe.

Dr. Fernando Pacheco, Ali's personal physician

For the parent of a Little Leaguer, a baseball game is simply a nervous breakdown divided into innings.

Earl Wilson

His greatest dream is to die in his own arms.

Irving Rudd, boxing promoter, on Hector Camacho, 1987

How would you like it if you were out on your job or in your office and you made a little mistake? And suddenly a bright red light flashed behind you and then 18,000 people started screaming, "Pig! Stupid ! Get that bum out of there."

Jacques Plante, New York Rangers goalie, on hockey fans

On the day of the race, a lot of people want you to sign something just before you get in the car so that they can say they got your last autograph.

A. J. Foyt, racecar driver

I never cease to amaze myself. I say this humbly.

Don King

Statistics are about as interesting as first-base coaches.

Jim Bouton

Baseball is very big with my people. It figures. It's the only time we can get to shake a bat at a white man without ·starting a riot.

Dick Gregory

They go on and on. It's like a guy telling a bad joke for fifteen minutes.

Tom Heinson, Boston Celtics coach, on the NBA playoffs

It was nice to see that Pinky Lee's estate has been settled.

Bob Costas, on a sports coat worn by Alabama basketball coach Wimp Sanderson, 1987

Eliminate the referees, raise the basket four feet, double the size of the basketball, limit the height of the players to 5′ 9″, bring back the center jump, let taxi drivers in free, and allow the players to carry guns.

Al McGuire, on how to make basketball more exciting

Yeah, but I love you more than football and basketball.

Tommy Lasorda, Dodgers manager, to his wife when she claimed he loved baseball and the Dodgers more than he loved her, 1986

Haven't they suffered enough?

Beano Cook, CBS sports publicist, upon learning that Bowie Kuhn had given the fifty-two former Iran hostages lifetime major league baseball passes, 1981

I knew I was in for a long year when we lined up for the national anthem on opening day and one of my players said, ''Every time I hear that song I have a bad game.''

Jim Leyland, Pittsburgh Pirates manager, 1987

The Angels are the first team I've ever been on where I feel I belong. They're all nuts, too.

Jimmy Piersall, Los Angeles Angels outfielder

Baseball isn't a business, it's more like a disease.

Walter O'Malley

Playing baseball for a living is like having a license to steal.

Pete Rose

Grantland Rice, the great sports writer, once said, "It's not whether you win or lose, it's how you played the game." Well, Grantland Rice can go to hell as far as I'm concerned.

Gene Autry, as California Angels manager

It's not whether you win or lose, but who gets the blame.

Blaine Nye, Dallas Cowboys lineman

A baseball manager is a necessary evil.

Sparky Anderson

Any ballplayer that don't sign autographs for little kids ain't American. He's a Communist.

Roger Hornsby, St. Louis Cardinals infielder

There isn't enough mustard in America to cover that hot dog.

Darold Knowles, on Reggie Jackson

The two of them deserve each other. One's a born liar and the other's convicted.

Billy Martin, on Reggie Jackson and George Steinbrenner

Last year I was assaulted by George Steinbrenner's Nazis, his Brown Shirts. He brainwashes those kids over there and they're led by Billy Martin— Hermann Goering II. They've got a convicted felon running the club. What else do you expect?

Bill Lee, Boston Red Sox pitcher, on a 1977 fight with the New York Yankees

Nothing's more limited than being a limited partner of George's.

John McMullen, Houston Astros owner, on his former limited partnership with George Steinbrenner, 1980

He treated us all the same—like dogs.

Jerry Kramer, of the Green Bay Packers, on coach Vince Lombardi

Football is the only game you come into with a semblance of intelligence and end up a babbling moron.

Mike Adamie, New York Jets running back

If it's such an important game, why are they playing it again next year?

Duane Thomas, Dallas Cowboys running back, on the Super Bowl

College football today is one of the last great strongholds of genuine old-fashioned American hypocrisy.

Paul Gallico

There's something about football that no other game has. There's sort of a mystique about it. It's a game in which you can feel a clean hatred for your opponent.

Ronald Reagan

Wendell doesn't know the meaning of the word fear, but then he doesn't know the meaning of most words.

Babe McCarthy, Kentucky Colonels coach, on basketball forward Wendell Ladner

I left because of illness and fatigue. The fans were sick and tired of me.

John Ralston, Denver Broncos coach, upon being fired

If their IQs were five points lower, they'd be geraniums.

Russ Francis, New England Patriots, on football players

If you play in New York long enough, you're bound to be an asshole.

Bill Russell, Los Angeles Dodgers shortstop, 1978

Football is a game designed to keep coal miners off the streets.

Jimmy Breslin

It was hard to have a conversation with anyone, there were so many people talking.

Yogi Berra, on a White House dinner he had attended, 1985

The football season is like pain. You forget how terrible it is until it seizes you again.

Sally Quinn

A former teammate of mine told me that we have, as a team, the collective intelligence of an orangutan. I cannot say that I disagree.

Phil Jackson, New York Knicks forward

We'd hand them a caramel candy, and if they took the wrapper off before they ate it, they'd get a basketball scholarship. If they ate the caramel with the paper still on it, we'd give them a football scholarship.

Frank Layden, former New Orleans Jazz coach, on a test he used to administer when he coached at Niagara, 1988

The only thing in this country that blacks really dominate, except for poverty, is basketball.

Al McGuire, Marquette basketball coach

Playing in the NBA isn't a beauty contest. They're all ugly.

Al Menendez, New Jersey Nets scout, on players and recruits

All that fancy stuff and they call it magic. I've been doing if for years and they call it school yard.

Joe Bryant, San Diego Clippers forward, on "Magic" Johnson

I consider playing basketball . . . the most shallow thing in the world.

Bill Russell

You can always tell Notre Dame grads. They're the ones who pick their nose just to show you their ring.

Al McGuire, NBC basketball analyst, 1985

Every obnoxious fan has a wife home who dominates him.

Al McGuire

Show me a good loser and I'll show you an idiot.

Leo Durocher

Our job is to raise the human race. Men have gotta catch up to us. And they've got about a million years to go.

Roseanne Barr, 1989

Whenever a friend succeeds,
something within me dies.

Gore Vidal

[I'm] not fit for human consumption
right now. Botulism . . . bad meat in a
can.

**Sylvester Stallone, on why he's
avoiding sexual entanglements,
1989**

I think that a society that condones
vaginal deodorant is a society in real
trouble.

**John Peel, BBC radio
announcer, 1985**

It's a piece of garbage.

**Donald Trump, on *Spy*
magazine, 1990**

All my contemporaries are assholes.

Paul Cezanne

I've never met a successful person
who wasn't neurotic.

Donald Trump, 1990

Gossip is the opiate of the oppressed.

Erica Jong, 1973

[Leona Helmsley] is a vicious, horrible
woman who systematically destroyed
the Helmsley name. . . . She set the
women's movement back fifty years.
She is a living nightmare, and to be
married to her must be like living in
hell.

Donald Trump, 1990

So OK, youth must be served; but
does it always have to be a meal for
cannibals?

Harlan Ellison, 1985

My friends tell me I have to be more
feminine, I have to be more ladylike;
but I just say, "Hey, suck my dick!"

**Roseanne Barr, as quoted by
Eddie Murphy, 1990**

The Wicked Witch of the West

**Ed Koch, on Leona Helmsley,
1989**

It's good girls who keep diaries—bad
girls don't have the time.

Roseanne Barr

It's not that I have any negative views on women. You just kind of have to keep them in place. If that means tossing them in the dumpster, then that's what you've got to do.
Morris Day, 1985

I never intend to look a day over twenty-eight, but it's going to cost Donald a lot of money.
Ivana Trump

I'm so sick of women. I hate women. Women are bitches. They're horrible. They're great to be friends with, they're horrible to be involved with.
Sandra Bernhard, 1989

I was led to believe I wasn't responsible for birth control. It was a communications situation there.
Steve Garvey, on impregnating a number of would-be brides, 1989

Look at the path of destruction he has left, and he's still smiling at the cameras. Steve is now blaming the women involved, and I find that appalling. . . . the guy is a sociopath. He doesn't have the same level of conscience as most men.
Cyndy Garvey, on ex-husband Steve Garvey, 1989

I'm pro-heterosexual. I can't get enough of women. I have sex as often as possible. . . . It's really hard to maintain a one-on-one relationship if the other person is not going to allow me to be with other people.

Axl Rose of Guns N' Roses, 1989

I personally prefer to look at a nude woman in a photo than a nude guy. I think it's no put-down to pose that way. I think the women who resent it are those who are afraid to admit they couldn't get into *Playboy*.

Barbi Benton

My reaction to porno films is as follows: After the first ten minutes, I want to go home and screw. After the first twenty minutes, I never want to screw again as long as I live.

Erica Jong, 1983

Cosmetics is a boon to every woman, but a girl's best beauty aid is still a near-sighted man.

Yoko Ono

If you're [a woman] in the public eye, the greatest problem you're going to have is that the men you attract are going to feel castrated.
Lucille Ball

I like to hurt women when I make love to them. . . . I like to hear them scream with pain, to see them bleed. . . . It gives me pleasure.
Mike Tyson

There's really no reason to have women on tour unless they've got a job to do. The only other reason is to screw. Otherwise they get bored. They just sit around and moan.
Mick Jagger

I'm very much in love with a woman, but I don't want her to know. If she knows I'm in love with her, she'll start treating me like shit. That's how women are.
Arsenio Hall, 1989

We don't believe in Women's Lib.
Leonard Haze of Yesterday & Today

We're all male chauvinists.
Joe Alves of Yesterday & Today

I hate contraception. . . . There's nothing I abhor more than planned parenthood. I'd rather have those fucking Communists over here.
Norman Mailer

I didn't know how to wear a tampon, and I thought if I wasn't a virgin, maybe they'd fit better.
Valerie Bertinelli, on why she lost her virginity

A full bosom is actually a millstone around a woman's neck. . . . [Breasts] are not parts of a person but lures slung around her neck, to be kneaded and twisted like magic putty, or mumbled and mouthed like lolly ices.
Germaine Greer, 1971

I've found that friendship between two women and those between a gay man and woman are closer then those a woman could have with a straight man. Straight men don't have the time to spend with you because they have to get laid, they have to work, and if they're married, they have to keep their marriage together.
Bette Midler, 1989

I would guess that most men who understand women at all feel hostility toward them. At their worst, women are low, sloppy beasts.

Norman Mailer

It's okay.

Jon Bon Jovi, on married life

Time Out asked me if I'm a committed drag queen or not, which pissed me off. Committed? What's committed? How can you be committed to a pair of falsies and stilettos?

Boy George, 1984

I could go to a restaurant, sit down at a table, and, if the waiter looked like he was really gay, I wouldn't eat my food.

Heavy metalist Thor, 1985

Get a very well-known, popular gay waiter. I don't give a shit what you think about gays. There's money involved.

Al "Grampa Munster" Lewis, on how to open a successful restaurant

I knew a good loser once; he was a queer.

Barry Goldwater, 1965

I had a nightmare that I'd be attacked by gays.

Harry Carson, New York Giants linebacker, on why he's afraid of being hospitalized in San Francisco

Rock and roll wives . . . I hate 'em. Fortunately, there's only a couple of 'em around, but honestly, I don't know how they have the nerve to continue in the face of their appalling failure.

Mick Jagger

I am very much in love with my wife and my wife's dog.

S. I. Newhouse

He called me for a divorce on the phone. . . . He said, "This will only take a minute . . . ."

Angie Dickinson, on ex-husband Burt Bacharach, 1989

I love women, every kind in existence . . . I can change their whole life in an instant. You put something in front of them that they can't stop eating, and boy, you got somebody's heart. I mean, you can start fooling around immediately—with complete power.

Chef Paul Prudhomme, 1989

Do you know why God created women? Because sheep can't type.

Kenneth Armbrister, Texas state senator

Women are great. When they dig you, there's nothing they won't do. That kind of loyalty is hard to find—unless you've got a good dog.

David Lee Roth

I prefer making love with a girl instead of a dog.

Klaus Meine of The Scorpions

My husband says my life is wasted on me.

Bette Midler, 1989

Tolerate men.

Katharine Hepburn, when asked, "What can women do better than men?", 1989

Love is a publicity stunt.

Louise Brooks

She came begging me to marry her. How could I turn the poor girl down?

Bryan Brown, on his courtship and marriage to Rachel Ward on the set of *The Thorn Birds*

Eaten up with guilt, shame, fears, and insecurities and obtaining, if he's lucky, a barely perceptible feeling, the male is, nonetheless, obsessed with screwing; he'll swim a river of snot, wade nostril-deep through a mile of vomit, if he thinks there'll be a friendly pussy awaiting him. Every man, deep down, knows he's a worthless piece of shit.

Valerie Solanas, would-be assassin of Andy Warhol, who emptied most of a .32 revolver into his chest at 7:30 P.M. on June 3, 1968, and subsequently achieved just slightly more attention in the national press than the "fifteen minutes" allotted to everyone by her target

I don't like the size of them; the scale is all wrong. The heads tend to be too big for the bodies and the hands and feet are a disaster and they keep falling into things . . . they should be neither seen nor heard. And no one must make another one.

Gore Vidal, on children, 1975

My parents love the new girlfriend and the new lifestyle. They even had me as a houseguest for a couple of weeks. They let me in the house. Gee, I think that's important.

Iggy Pop

I'd never even picked up a baby before I had one. I just thought they were like a load of Martians.

Chrissie Hynde

Sometimes a woman can really persuade you to make an asshole of yourself.

Rod Stewart, 1982

A man in love is incomplete until he's married—then he's finished.

Zsa Zsa Gabor

You cowboys are all faggots.

Sid Vicious, to Texas audience, 1978

I don't think men's bodies look good in the nude at all.

Samantha Fox, 1986

You can't trust politicians. It doesn't matter to me who makes a political speech. It's all lies . . . and it applies to any rock star who wants to make a political speech as well.

Bob Geldof, 1978

The system want pure love songs like ol' Frank Sinatra, they do't want not'ing wit' no protest. It makes too much trouble.

Bob Marley, 1978

A government can make people look like fools.

Clint Eastwood, 1985

What's an actor who played with a monkey in a movie want to be doing in politics?

Ronald Reagan to Clint Eastwood upon the latter's election as Mayor of Carmel, California, 1986

Yecch.

Ed Koch, on Mario Cuomo

Moron.

Donald Trump, on Ed Koch

Let him get a job like every other guy. Just go to work, W-O-R-K, which he hasn't done as mayor. . . . If he doesn't get a job, he should retire to Florida.

Jimmy Breslin, on Ed Koch, 1988

It's nothing, it's wasting your life. . . . This rural America thing—I'm telling you, it's a joke.

Ed Koch, on outside the city life

He should go to a spa and lose some ego.

Bella Abzug, former New York congresswoman, on Ed Koch

He searches through each day and night for a safe stage, where he can talk mindlessly, or, covering himself with spangles, dance and sing.

Jimmy Breslin, on Ed Koch

Piggy, piggy, piggy.

Ed Koch, on Donald Trump

Bess might get a nice job shopping. She'd be a great personal shopper.

Tama Janowitz, on Bess Myerson, 1988

Since the masses have always known we are far from impoverished, it would have been a terrible mistake for me to have appeared before them in old or shabby clothes just because they dress shabbily. . . . They would have thought I was belittling them. On the other hand, it flattered them to no end to see that I always took the trouble to wear my best *ternos*—I would even wear dangling earrings to make them feel important.

Imelda Marcos

Eisenhower didn't know anything when he became President, and in his years in office, he didn't learn anything.

Harry Truman

Nonaction was characteristic of Eisenhower as President because he'd proved to be such a dumb son-of-a-bitch when he got out of his general's uniform.

Harry Truman

Eisenhower was too chickenhearted to be vindictive.

Harry Truman

Fourteen heart attacks, and he had to die in my week. In *my* week.

Janis Joplin, on losing the *Newsweek* cover story to Eisenhower's death

Any political party that can't cough up anything better than a treacherous brain-damaged old vulture like Hubert Humphrey deserves every beating it gets. They don't hardly make 'em like Hubert any more—but just to be on the safe side, he should be castrated anyway.

Hunter Thompson, author/ journalist

There is no way to grasp what a shallow, contemptible, and hopelessly dishonest old hack Hubert Humphrey really is until you've followed him around for a while on the campaign trail.

Hunter Thompson, author/ journalist

They're not like the folks you were reared with.

Lyndon Johnson, on foreigners, 1967

I don't know fuck about the UN. I'd rather sing about rock and roll and chicks.

Tom Petty

I read someplace that suicide rates are very high in Vermont—they must be sick of cutting all that grass.

Stokely Carmichael, 1967

The Grateful Dead should be sponsored by the government—a public service. And they should set us up to play at places that need to get high.

Jerry Garcia

If I'd still been President when Fidel Castro started that revolution . . . I'd have picked up the phone and made friends with him. . . . I'd have said, "Listen, Fidel, come on down here to Washington and let's talk." Maybe I'd have hinted that it would be nice if he took a haircut and a good shower before he came.

Harry Truman

Well, he would have made a very good bartender.

Gore Vidal, on Ted Kennedy

I used to have a hunch that [George] Wallace was going to pick Elvis as his running mate. If he'd done that I think he would have picked up five more states. Most people would pick Elvis over Reagan. I would.

Phil Ochs

He will probably be President . . . I think he's very shrewd, but I think he's absolutely cold. I think he may prove to be, well, very dangerous.

James Baldwin, on Robert Kennedy, 1968

All you have to do is to be black and don't curse the Jews directly and the Jew will vote for a black in a second.

Jackie Mason, 1989

A fancy schvartze with a mustache.

**Jackie Mason, on David
Dinkins, 1989**

He's the sick Jewish problem.

**Ira Silverman, executive V.P.,
American Jewish Committee,
on Jackie Mason's comments
on David Dinkins, 1989**

Most Americans think of politics as little more than the game show that is broadcast just before "Wheel of Fortune." In the real world, *none* of these guys, in either party, has achieved the name identification, the popularity, or perhaps even the credibility of Vanna White.

**Journalist Joe Klein, on the
1988 presidential race**

Another thing about my mother that's really intriguing: On the day that Bobby Kennedy was killed, she bought a horse, and then she wanted to name it Sirhan Sirhan, but the Jockey Club wouldn't permit it. Isn't that strange?

**Patty Hearst, on her mother,
Catherine Hearst, 1974**

What do you think about the CIA? What does Daddy always tell you about the CIA? Doesn't Daddy always say, when he picks up the phone, "The CIA sucks"?

**Peter Fonda, to his daughter
Bridget, ca. 1967**

In Czechoslovakia, there is no such thing as freedom of the press. In the United States, there is no such thing as freedom from the press.

Martina Navrhitilova

I don't have one nostalgic bone in my body for the 1960s.

Timothy Leary, 1976

There's something pompous about people who join peace movements.
. . . They're the radical equivalent of working for the FBI.

Norman Mailer

Setting fire to yourself is not the answer. With my luck, I would be uninflammable.

**Woody Allen, on protesting for
peace, ca. mid-1960s**

That's my personal hang-up, that all the rich should be killed.

**Howie Klein, San Francisco
punk club manager**

The day I vote for a Reagan or a Bush is the day I shoot my mother.

Actor John Cusack, 1989

. . . to show up those cheap Texas broads.

John F. Kennedy, on how Jackie Kennedy should dress for their trip to Dallas in November 1963

She hated my father and she can't stand it that his children turned out so much better than hers.

John F. Kennedy, on Eleanor Roosevelt's opposition to his presidential candidacy

Tell me something nice about Kennedy so I can get excited about him.

Shelley Winters, on John F. Kennedy, at the 1960 Democratic Convention

It is almost as if he had never called businessmen sons of bitches, sent the troops to Ole Miss, the refugees to the Bay of Pigs, or kicked the budget sky-high.

Tom Wicker, on John F. Kennedy

The only thing that could possibly save British politics would be Margaret Thatcher's assassin.

Morrissey of The Smiths, 1984

When, years later, she married Rumpelstiltskin, I felt like a child discovering, in his father's drawer, the Santa Claus suit.

Joyce Maynard, on Jackie Kennedy's marriage to Aristotle Onassis

Oh, fuck Jerry Rubin. For chrissake, Jerry and Abby Hoffman will probably be doing a vaudeville show ten years from now! Look at those characters in the Conspiracy Seven! They couldn't organize a luncheon, let alone a social revolution.

Saul Alinsky, political analyst, 1971

This is the Age of Brand Names. . . . Andy Warhol himself is a brand name. Bobby Kennedy was a brand name. Campaign promises are advertising claims. Voters are consumers. The United States has an obligation to Israel, and Ajax is stronger than dirt. Bobby Kennedy was the White Knight. And somebody out there in television-land didn't like his cleansing agent. And gave him Excedrin Headache Infinity.

Paul Krassner, radical journalist and humorist, 1968

Chet Huntley cried when he reported the death of Martin Luther King. I never saw him cry when, week after week after week, he delivered the latest body count from Vietnam as if it were a grocery list.

Paul Krassner, 1968

I dreamed the devil appeared the other night and wanted to make a bargain for my soul and the William Morris Agency handled the deal. They got me damned to hell for eternity—with options.

Woody Allen

Anybody naive enough to think they're going into the army to learn a trade deserves to get their head blown off.

Fad Gadget, 1982

They've taken all the romance out of divorce.

Raoul Felder, New York divorce lawyer, on the changes in divorce law, 1988

He was born to be a salesman. He would be an admirable representative of Rolls-Royce. But an ex-king cannot start selling motorcars.

The Duchess of Windsor, on the Duke of Windsor

Such an active lass. So outdoorsy. She loves nature in spite of what it did to her.

Bette Midler, on Princess Anne of England

[She looks] as if she makes beds in Ireland or milks cows . . . [and she] walks like a duck with a bad leg.

Richard Blackwell, fashion designer, on the Duchess of York, Sarah Ferguson, 1988

A triumph of the embalmer's art.

Gore Vidal, on Ronald Reagan

That ex-husband of Jane Wyman's. Remember what she said about him? Don't ask him what time it is, or he'll tell you how to make a watch.

Henny (Mrs. Jim) Backus, on Ronald Reagan

I think politics is an instrument of the Devil.

Bob Dylan

Bob Dole is an organ transplant that the body politic in New Hampshire is slowly rejecting.

John Buckley, press secretary to Jack Kemp, 1988

Babs Bush . . . reads *House and Garden* for fashion tips.

Judy Tenuta, on Barbara Bush

Reagan is by no means a bad actor, but he would hardly be convincing, I said, as a presidential candidate [in *The Best Man*]. If I had cast Reagan in the role, it would have sated his appetite for the Presidency, and we'd be much better off.

Gore Vidal

Richard Nixon impeached himself. He gave us Gerald Ford as his revenge.

Bella Abzug

I support Wallace about as much as your average American supported Hitler.

Leon Wilkeson, of Lynyrd Skynrd, on being named Honorary Lieutenant Colonel in the Alabama State Militia by George Wallace

I'd rather be Roosevelt in a wheelchair than Reagan on a horse.

Jesse Jackson, 1988

He says his lust is in his heart. I hope it's a little lower.

Shirley Maclaine, on Jimmy Carter

It must mean that he's as dull as his first wife, Jane Wyman, said he was.

Bette Davis, on Ronald Reagan's "stainless reputation"

For a working man or woman to vote Republican this year is the same as a chicken voting for Colonel Sanders.

Walter Mondale, 1983

You can't always support the weak. You have to make the weak stand up on one leg, or half a leg, whatever they've got.

Neil Young, on his support of Ronald Reagan, 1984

The smell of [Henry Kissinger's] dirty socks was overpowered by his denture breath.

Mamie Van Doren

If you think wealth determines genius and poverty otherwise, then look at Dan Quayle and look at me.

Jesse Jackson

To be honest with you, I think that the working class are as bigoted and conservative as the other classes anyway. In fact, the working-class mentality is pretty stupid.

Graham Parker, 1978

If I were married to her, I'd be sure to have dinner ready when she got home.

George Shultz, on Margaret Thatcher

Truman Capote has made lying an art. A *minor* art.

Gore Vidal, 1977

I find intellectuals are more interested in gossip than anybody else.

Dorothy Schiff, past publisher of the *New York Post*

The somewhat puffy cheeks and vulnerable mouth and chin complete the expression of a sick wildcat caught in a parlor.

Cecil Beaton, on Carson McCullers

Some editors are failed writers, but so are most writers.

T. S. Eliot

A good many young writers make the mistake of enclosing a stamped, self-addressed envelope, big enough for the manuscript to come back in. This is too much of a temptation for the editor.

Ring Lardner

An editor is one who separates the wheat from the chaff and prints the chaff.

Adlai Stevenson

I know only a few things. I've had a few *major* experiences. I'm no Shakespeare, no Hugo, no Balzac. Something a little higher than a louse. That's not overestimating myself, is it?

Henry Miller

It's a damn good story. If you have any comments, write them on the back of a check.

Erle Stanley Gardner; note on a manuscript sent to a hard-to-please magazine editor

Yevgeny Yevtushenko is the Soviet equivalent of Rod McKuen.

New York writer Earl H. Dedview, Jr.

I never read a word of Hemingway, I've never read any F. Scott Fitzgerald. I certainly never read any fucking Shakespeare.

Syndicated columnist Bob Greene, 1977

I think Shakespeare is shit. Absolute shit! He may have been a genius for his time, but I just can't relate to that stuff. "Thee" and "thou"—the guy sounds like a faggot.

Gene Simmons of Kiss

In my mind there is something silly about a man who wears a white suit all the time, especially in New York.

Norman Mailer, on Tom Wolfe

The thinking man's redneck.

Mary Gordon, on Tom Wolfe

If my books had been any worse, I should not have been invited to Hollywood. If they had been any better, I should not have come.

Raymond Chandler

I wrote a big American novel. Where's the hi-fi? Where's the stereo?

Nelson Algren, author of *Man with the Golden Arm*

That's not writing, that's typing.

Truman Capote, on the work of Jack Kerouac, 1963

Some of us here have been thinking that it might be a good thing for you to hear the clank of iron.

Mark Van Doren to Allen Ginsberg, on the latter's activities while a student at Columbia University

You had a choice of either being a knave or a fool, and you seem to have opted for both.

John Simon to Erich Segal

A bad writer, overrated, a dishonest writer . . . every word she writes is a lie, including "and" and "the."

Mary McCarthy, on Lillian Hellman

An abominably written book. . . . There are roles in plays called actor-proof. They are so conceived that even the worst actor will do fairly well. So *Another Country* is writer-proof.

Norman Mailer, on James Baldwin's novel, 1963

Mailer . . . decocts matters of the first philosophical magnitude from an examination of his own ordure, and I am not talking about his books.

William F. Buckley, Jr., on Norman Mailer, 1968

I've read forty pages actually, after which I couldn't stomach any more. I mean, how many swallows of a rotten stew do I have to swallow before I puke?

John Simon, on Jacqueline Susann's *Valley of the Dolls*, 1969

If I had an affair with Jack the Ripper, the offspring would be Rex Reed.

Jacqueline Susann

I think James Joyce is a bore. *Ulysses* is a bore. . . . Nabokov and I are on the same level.

Jacqueline Susann

If James Joyce had walked in, somebody would have called him ''Baby.''

Dick Schaap, on Earl Wilson's publicity party for Jacqueline Susann's *Valley of the Dolls*

I think Philip Roth is a great writer. But I wouldn't want to shake his hand.

Jacqueline Susann

A born transvestite . . . a truck driver in drag.

Truman Capote, on Jacqueline Susann, 1969

Every generation gets the Tiny Tim that it deserves.

Gore Vidal, on Truman Capote

Piece by piece, line by line, and without interruption, worthless.

Renata Adler, on Pauline Kael's writing

All a writer has to do to get a woman is to say he's a writer. It's an aphrodisiac.

Saul Bellow, 1976

Writers are always selling somebody out.

Joan Didion, 1968

Pollack? Socially, he was a real jerk. Very unpleasant to be around. Very stupid. . . . and he always got completely drunk, and he made a point of behaving badly to everyone. . . . he was a star painter all right, but that's no reason to pretend he was a pleasant person. . . . I'll tell you what kind of person he was. He would go over to a black person and say, "How do you like your skin color?" or he'd ask a homosexual, "Sucked any cocks lately?"

Larry Rivers, on Jackson Pollack

I can't see the point of those drips, and I think he couldn't do anything else particularly well.

Francis Bacon, on Jackson Pollack, 1989

Abstract art? A product of the untalented, sold by the unprincipled to the utterly bewildered.

Al Capp

There's a big difference between *The Merchant of Venice* and a photograph of two males of different races . . . on a marble-top table. I'm embarrassed to even talk to you about this. I'm embarrassed to talk to my wife.

Jesse Helms, on Robert Mapplethorpe's photographs

He's arrogant and imbued with self-importance.

Leo Castelli, on Julian Schnabel

What's so great about Broadway? It's as hardhearted as Hollywood. . . . Most plays spend three hours on the problem of whether somebody is going to get laid or not, and you know as well as I do it's not that big a problem.

George Peppard

It's like being in jail.

Madonna, on being a stage actor, 1988

I hate the theater.

Michelangelo Antonioni

What do dancers think of Fred Astaire? It's no secret. We hate him. He gives us a complex because he's too perfect. His perfection is an absurdity. It's too hard to face.

Mikhail Baryshnikov

Cartoon classical music.

Stewart Copeland, on opera, 1989

When an opera star sings her head off, she usually improves her appearance.

Victor Borge

I said to my boyfriend Arnie, "Ya gotta kiss me where it smells" —so he drove me to Wapping.

Bette Midler, 1978

New York? Who'd want to live there? It's like living on top of a rotting corpse, vampire life. You crawl out of your coffin and go into the decaying streets—and get shot at.

Singer John Hiatt, 1982

A bowl of underpants.

Don Van Vliet, a.k.a. Captain Beefheart, on New York City

There's no more crime in New York— there's nothing left to steal.

Henny Youngman

Living in New York City gives people real incentives to want things that nobody else wants.

Andy Warhol

This muck heaves and palpitates. It is multidirectional and has a mayor.

Donald Barthelme, on New York City

New York is a place where the rich walk, the poor drive Cadillacs, and beggars die of malnutrition with thousands of dollars in their mattresses.

Duke Ellington

There is no greenery. It is enough to make a stone sad.

Nikita Krhushchev, on New York City, 1964

New York is a city of terribly lonely people who can get together only when they're drugged or drunk or in bed.

Rollo May

Lovers in New York don't turn against it . . . because of taxes or crime or decaying public services. They do it because their happiness here is so dependent on illusions, and their illusions collapse.

Kurt Vonnegut

Hollywood is a place where they'll pay you ten thousand dollars for a kiss and fifty cents for your soul.

Marilyn Monroe

Working in Hollywood gives one a certain expertise in the field of prostitution.

Jane Fonda

In Hollywood, if you don't have happiness, you send out for it.

Rex Reed

I mean, who would want to live in a place where the only cultural advantage is that you can turn on a red light?

Woody Allen, on Los Angeles, 1977

In California, in the cool night air, you even felt healthy when you puked—it was so different from New York.

Andy Warhol

The biggest attraction in LA is to sit around the swimming pool. I can't stand that. You sit there covered in oil, you try to read but you can't because the pages stick together, and when you dive into the pool there's this slick on the water because all the lotion's washed off. I don't have to worry about that in London because no one has a tan.

Bob Hoskins, 1989

LA's okay, I guess, if you wanna be the bronzed Goddess, driving around in your Cherokee jeep, in your satin shorts, with your asshole jerk-off rock 'n' roll star boyfriend, with his shorts full of cocaine . . .

Chrissie Hynde, of The Pretenders, 1981

It is like Mexican cooking without chili, or Chinese egg rolls missing their mustard.

Norman Mailer, on Los Angeles

In England, you know, you can become famous for doing absolutely nothing. . . . London is the only city in the world that is run entirely on bullshit.

Boy George, 1989

Not as bad as playing Akron.

George Burns, after waking from heart-bypass surgery, 1974

I can't wait for this city to rot. I can't wait to see weeds growing through empty streets.

Jean Genet, on Chicago, 1968

Why can't we tour places where they speak English and serve decent beer?

Terry Chambers, of XTC, on their tour of Venezuela, 1981

Your constant belittling of America makes you Brits seem like mindless idiots, which we have always suspected you were.

Lisa Lisa in letter to *Melody Maker*, 1988

You could call this opium land. This area is full of creative artists of one-time great promise—hot shots from New York, Chicago, or wherever, who came out to San Francisco, attracted by the press, and every ten years there's some kind of insane social revolution happening around here anyway. Somewhere along the way they seem to forget that creative drive they had, and just hang out for ten or twelve years, just smoking grass.

Drummer Nick Gravenites, on San Francisco

In America, life is one long expectoration.

Oscar Wilde

London's a kind of massive souvenir shop, a facade of how London used to be. It just isn't English anymore. It seems very Americanized, which is something to dwell upon with horror.

Morrissey, of The Smiths, 1983

It is sung, played, and written for the most part by cretinous goons and by means of its almost imbecilic reiterations and sly, lewd—in plain fact, dirty lyrics . . . it manages to be the martial music of every sideburned delinquent on the face of the earth. This rancid-smelling aphrodisiac I deplore.

I'm a fairly with-it person, but this stuff is curling my hair.

Tipper Gore, wife of Tennessee senator Albert Gore, on the need for cleaning up rock and roll, 1985

Rock has always been the Devil's music.

David Bowie

Take the cock out of rock and it's nothing. It's not relevant.

Don McLean, 1973

I think rock and roll is a good medium that hasn't really been used to full advantage. It isn't exactly like TV, of course, but I think that if your message is strong enough it can have as much impact as . . . a Wella Balsam commercial.

Ric Gallagher

Commercial rock and roll music is a brutalization of one stream of contemporary Negro church music . . . an obscene looting of a cultural expression.

Ralph Ellison, 1964

You have to blame Thomas Alva Edison for today's rock and roll. He invented electricity.

Stan Getz

No amount of electronic amplification can turn a belch into an aria.

Alan Jay Lerner, on rock and roll, 1978

The majority of pop stars are complete idiots in every respect.

Sade, 1985

Rock music is at the stage where it has become part of the establishment . . . How can you be a rebel, when rebellion is the norm? Therefore rock 'n' roll has lost its power as a revolutionary force. I think the bands who call themselves revolutionary are playing at it. They're having no effect whatsoever.

Sting, 1982

Motown was the sixties, and that's the problem with Motown. They think they're still *in* the sixties. They're not, and they gotta cater for the people in the street. All the old Supremes fans are winos with false teeth.

Rick James, 1984

Those kids don't know anything. They're lying around in mud listening to a shitty sound system and eating day-old garbage, and they think they're having a good time. They're just being had, mister, had.

Bill Graham, on rock festivals

I bet he's about four foot three. I bet he's got boogies up his nose. I bet his feet are small.

Elton John, on *NY Times* critic John Rockwell

Can you imagine working for a fucking year and you get a "B-plus" from an asshole in the *Village Voice?*

Lou Reed, on critic Robert Christgau

Tell Dave I'm not upset and I'll be happy to sell him an album this year to review.

Steve Martin, on Dave Marsh's panning of his record

I don't read the music papers much, y'know. They're full of people that think they're literary geniuses, putting things in brackets 'cos they've just read a bit of Thomas Pynchon.

Graham Parker, 1982

Who is Jon Pareles, and why is he writing pseudo-liberal hogwash for the *New York Times?*

Sean Penn, on Pareles' review of Guns N' Roses and Public Enemy, 1989

Rock journalism is people who can't write interviewing people who can't talk for people who can't read.

Frank Zappa, 1978

When I'm writing songs, the minutes are like hours. I sit there with nothing—just a big picture of Greil Marcus in my head hanging over the piano.

Randy Newman, on critics

It's going to rub off somewhere. Otherwise, I might as well have been deaf.

Drummer Jason Bonham, on the influence of his father John's band, Led Zeppelin

As a rule, musicians are not fun.

Gail Zappa

I'm just not attracted to guys with beards. Maybe that's why Jesus bores me. Maybe if he shaved I'd dig him.

Patti Smith, 1977

The most difficult time [I have] is waking up in the morning and facing reality. . . . when I hear the birds singing, I think, "Is that me?"

Brian Wilson, on himself

If I could, I'd wring Carl's neck.

Brian Wilson, on his brother Carl

I'm scared of Gene. Obviously.

Brian Wilson, on his psychiatrist, Dr. Eugene Landy

I rued the day that the Beatles were unfortunately born into this world. They are, in my mind, responsible for most of the degradation that has happened, not only musically, but in the sense of youth orientation too.

Frank Sinatra, Jr.

The Beastie Boys are just dicks. Being successful won't change them. They'll always be dicks.

Russell Simmons, manager of The Beastie Boys, 1984

Censorship should not be a bad word. No society can survive without it. I believe that the stop sign at the corner is healthy censorship. That's what the Constitution had in mind—self-imposed, majority-approved censorship.

Pat Boone, 1985

You know, there's something about me that makes a lot of people want to throw up.

Pat Boone

He's a little too fairyish-looking for me. I guess it's because I'm American, but I don't like to see boys wearing makeup.

Patti Smith, on David Bowie

He has a great potential for true idleness.

Angela Bowie, on David Bowie

Jeff Beck is pathetic.

Pete Townshend, 1975

How come nobody ever asks Kris Kristofferson questions like that?

Bob Dylan, when asked how he imagines God, 1976

I've seen Stevie's show, I've seen Christine's show. To me, they both bordered on being lounge acts, simply because they were resting so heavily on Fleetwood Mac's laurels.

Lindsey Buckingham, on former Fleetwood Mac colleagues Stevie Nicks and Christine McVie

With all the great musicians in this town, why'd they have to fly Paul Shaffer in?

Robert Palmer, on the ground-breaking ceremony for the American Music Awards Hall of Fame, in Memphis, 1989

I think they'll still be debating whether she was pushed from that building, or jumped.

Don Was of Was Not Was, when asked what Debbie Gibson will be doing in twenty years

. . . I've met Iggy Pop and the guy's a sad, old pathetic shit. We went to a rehearsal studio and Johnny Rotten was there, and he was just this completely pathetic zero. He's a sad, old comedian. I thought, "Well, at least we've done more than that old fucking scumbag." Bowie is responsible for the worst side of the music.

Jim Reid, of Jesus & Mary Chain

I am a dork.

Iggy Pop, 1978

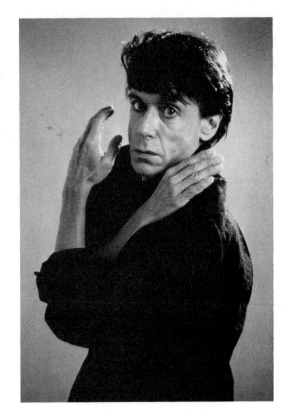

I wouldn't wish my career on a friend.

Fabian

Whether we're ahead or behind, we were never really a part of the world that is calling us a beached whale. We were never a part of it, we don't want to be now and we never will. Just fuck 'em.

Mickey Hart, drummer for The Grateful Dead

I feel as if I've been shitting without eating, intellectually. I'm just all shit and no food.

Grace Slick, on Jefferson Starship

It did seem impossible for her to go on . . . she would have needed a portable toilet on stage after every number.

Marty Balin of Jefferson Starship, on Grace Slick's departure from the group, 1978

I can't sing and throw up at the same time.

Grace Slick

The Grateful Dead are at least consistent; they remain the worst band in creation.

Dave Marsh, 1989

We want to be one of the great bands, not like The Grateful Dead.

Clem Burke, drummer for Blondie

The Dead is an imperfect band. We don't go out there and try to be perfect, because if we did then we would fail every time. In our very imperfection, we're perfect.

Mickey Hart, drummer for The Grateful Dead

I really feel like we did it our own way. We said "fuck you" then; I say "fuck you" now.

Mickey Hart, drummer for The Grateful Dead

We call Michael Jackson "Smelly" because he's so polite and proper, we can't even get him to say the word "funky."

Quincy Jones

I can't fathom Michael Jackson at all.

Morrissey of The Smiths, 1984

I hate it when she does that sexy stuff on stage. It makes me puke! Fuck Grace Slick? I wouldn't even let her *blow* me!

Marty Balin of Jefferson Starship

I really wanted to be Michael Jackson when I was growing up. But if I met him today, I'd unplug his oxygen tent, rip off his surgical mask and spit in his face.

Mike D, The Beastie Boys, 1987

The Beatles never had anything to say. It was always nice happy stuff. What *did* they ever say?

Lou Reed, 1973

Christianity will go. It will vanish and shrink. . . . We're more popular than Jesus now. I don't know which will go first—rock and roll or Christianity.

John Lennon

I hate disco music.

Barry Gibb

I've come to the realization that I have absolutely no idea what I'm doing half the time.

David Bowie, 1985

Bolan isn't camp—he's prissy, and fey, and engrossed in his own image.

David Bowie, 1972

We're fucking forty-four-year-old men, and we're behaving like children. It's silly, absolutely fucking idiotic. Retarded.

Eric Burdon, 1985

He should be the first guy indicted for crimes of such extreme pretension that he's actually physically jailed.

Bob Guccione, Jr., on David Byrne

He's a wimp.

Nikki Sixx of Motley Crue, on Jon Bon Jovi

What will Bob Dylan be doing in twenty years? To be truthful, who cares?

Andy Partridge of XTC

Dylan once said to Keith, "I could have written 'Satisfaction' but you couldn't have written 'Tambourine Man.' "

Mick Jagger, 1968

It's understandable to me, perhaps not to you, but I can only think of inconsequentially detrimental things to say about the emergence of lyrics from my various bodily orifices. "Substitute," for example, was written as a spoof of "Nineteenth Nervous Breakdown." On the demo I sang with an affected Jagger-like accent which Kit [The Who's manager] obviously liked, as he suggested the song as a follow-up to "My Generation." The lyric has come to be the most quoted Who lyric ever. It somehow goes to show that the "trust the art, not the artist" tag that people put on Dylan's silence about his work could be a good idea. To me, "Mighty Quinn" is about the five Perfect Masters of the age, the best of all being Meher Baba of course. To Dylan, it's probably about gathering, or the joys of placing dog shit in the garbage to foul up Alan J. Weberman.

Pete Townshend, 1970

I don't like Bob Dylan. I don't like his attitude or his records. All he stands for is a bad influence. Being cheeky with the press was bad. He says he's not a singer—so why does he sing? If he's going to be a public figure, he's got to be in the press. All that protest thing was a load of rubbish. I don't *hate* listening to his records, but I can't stand it when people say he's a genius. I just want to forget about that fellow.

Tom Jones, 1966

Duran Duran are completely disgusting, and crass, and offensive.

Mick Hucknall of Simply Red, 1985

I've already forgotten who Bob Dylan was.

Elvis Costello, 1978

I'm not saying this to be cool, but disco sucks—I mean, can you imagine some kid wanting to grow up and play on a Donna Summer album?

Lou Reed

Sometimes I think I'd like to have a huge disco hit, so that everybody would know who I am and the critics would hate me.

Chris Isaak, 1989

With my hands around a white man's neck.

Miles Davis, on "How he'd like to spend the last five minutes before he dies."

I think I can put together a better rock band than Jimi Hendrix.

Miles Davis, 1970

White folks ask me, "Was it fun?" I don't even know what fun is. That's such a corny expression. I never heard anybody black that I talk to or hang around with say, "Man, we had some fun!" What the fuck is fun? Black people just tell you what they did, but white folks say, "We had fun." I have never known what they meant.

Miles Davis, 1989

Groups like Genesis and Yes are about as exciting as a used Kleenex. It might as well be Tony Bennett.

Nick Lowe

I resent performing for fucking idiots who don't know anything.

John Lennon

John Lennon ain't no revolutionary— he's a fucking idiot.

Todd Rundgren, 1975

If I found her floating in my pool, I'd punish my dog.

Joan Rivers, on Yoko Ono, 1983

It's embarrassing for people to ask you what the name of your group is and you don't want to say it out loud.

Faye Hunter of Let's Active

I gave Otis Redding his start! I was his idol! I gave—you know Jimi Hendrix? I gave Jimi his start! He started out playing guitar with me in my band! I gave the Beatles their first tour! I gave the Stones their first tour! In England!

Little Richard

as good as she did back then. I don't like that. She should have aged some. She looks just like she did when she was twelve. I wonder if she can screw any better.

Jerry Lee Lewis, on Myra Lewis's book, 1989

Everyone that's walked into Jerry's life has either become a tragedy, a fatality, or a disruption.

Myra Lewis, on ex-husband, Jerry Lee Lewis

The worst piece of shit that I ever read, full of distorted lies. She was going to call that book *Balls of Fire*, but I said, "Myra, why not be honest about it?"—heh, heh, heh. Myra's still up and going, and she still looks

If I was still married to Jerry, I'd probably be dead now.

Myra Lewis

Just don't get too close to him and you won't get hurt.

Waylon Jennings, on Jerry Lee Lewis, 1978

I don't like no overdubbin'. When you're making love to a woman, ya can't go back and overdub.

Jerry Lee Lewis, 1978

They said I hated Jimmy McCullough's guts. What I really said is that he's a nasty little cunt. There's a big difference, you know.

Geoff Britten, Wings drummer, claiming he was misquoted in *Melody Maker*

Madonna reinforces everything absurd and offensive. Desperate womanhood. Madonna is closer to organized prostitution than anything else.

Morrissey of The Smiths, 1986

You think I'm an asshole now? You should've seen me when I was drunk.

John Cougar Mellencamp

If we were all devastatingly handsome and actually liked one another, we'd probably be Duran Duran or the biggest band on earth. As it is, I'm actually quite a decent chap, and the rest of the group are wankers.

Jools Holland, on Squeeze, 1985

Joni Mitchell is about as modest as Mussolini.

David Crosby

People talk to me about Carmel and Sade, and what do I think of the new jazz scene? *Jazz* scene? What are you fucking talking about?

Malcolm McLaren, 1984

I'd rather stick on a Billie Holiday record, and hear the job done properly.

Johnny Marr, guitarist of The Smiths, on Sade, 1984

[Malcolm McLaren] is just a conniving little shit. People see some sort of glamour in him being just a total bastard.

Johnny Rotten, 1978

It was all as inevitable as a fairy tale— like falling in love with King Arthur, or maybe it was more like falling in love with Darth Vader.

Patricia Kennealy, girlfriend of Jim Morrison

We're going to have a hell of a lot more freedom and space, because New Order is unlike INXS in that they don't try and deny us sound checks.

John Lydon, on touring with New Order, 1989

[Johnny] was a total waste of time, a *complete* fraud.

Malcolm McLaren, 1984

The man is a pathological liar.

Johnny Rotten, on Malcolm, 1984

Malcolm McLaren . . . the bourgeois anarchist. That just about sums him up.

Johnny Rotten, 1978

I didn't even feel sorry for him when he died.

Lou Reed, on Jim Morrison, 1977

In a word, I'm boring.

Randy Newman

Ozzy Osbourne is a moron; he couldn't carry a tune around in a suitcase.

Ronnie James Dio, of Black Sabbath, 1982

PIL sounds to me like Uriah Heep on Mandrax.

Joe Strummer of The Clash, 1982

I opened the door for a lot of people, and they just ran through and left me holding the knob.

Bo Diddley, 1971

Reggae is to me the most racist music in the world. It's an absolute total glorification of black supremacy.

Morrissey of The Smiths, 1986

I think it's pretty much the same everywhere. They adore us.

Sting, on whether fans like The Police better in America or England, 1983

These metal haircut bands all sound the same . . . I mean, isn't there more to life than money, cars, and [women]?

Michael Monroe, ex-frontman for Hanoi Rocks

Why do all heavy-metal guitarists look like Joan Jett?

Boy George

I really despised the idea that in order to be in a group and play hard music you had to be covered in your own vomit.

Morrissey of The Smiths, on British punk rock

It's funny about this punk rock thing. I don't know if it's me getting old or what, but I don't like it that much. It's too negative. I mean, it's just pure rot.

Pete Sears of The Jefferson Starship

A lot of us were brought up in the Catholic church and we hated nuns. I hated nuns.

Richie Detrick of The Nuns

If there's anything you can categorize, it's punks. They're the epitome of categorization, because they're completely one-dimensional. I love it, it's really back to where rock is at. As I was saying before, rock music really has no other intent. But I hate being lumped into it or compared with it.

Michael Cotten of The Tubes

I don't believe that their problems are that substantial. It all stems from England more than it does over here. They want to rip the rich people apart.

Aynsley Dunbar, drummer, on punk rock

There's a lot of Johnny Rotten's bastard children running the streets. They've been sold into bondage and it frightens me to see them. . . . They've been sold the image of violence and they've turned it into the *reality* of violence.

Bono, U2, 1982

In the end, I found most punks really gray and sexless. I'd rather dress up as Liberace.

Adam Ant, 1981

The Sex Pistols were terrible live, very unprofessional, very sloppy. Johnny Rotten came over to me and said, "What do you think?" And I said, "I thought you guys stunk"—so he said, "Well I think you stink, too."

Johnny Ramone, 1978

I was in a club, and a bunch of girls who didn't know who I was—but knew that I was somebody who maybe they should know—kept saying to me, "Boy, you're really weird, what do you do?" I was rather drunk at the time, so I said the first thing that came into my head. "Actually I used to be a male prostitute." They said, "Wow, what's your name?" . . . and I told them, "Simon Le Bon."

Marc Almond, 1982

Religion and punk rock don't mix.

Al Green

In my heart I feel Mexican-German. I feel if I were to organize it correctly, I would try to sing like a Mexican and think like a German. I get it mixed up sometimes anyway. I sing like a Nazi and I think like a Mexican and I can't get anything right.

Linda Ronstadt

Rock and roll is an antique. . . . America is selling an antiquated dream. With the exception of Vietnam, nothing's happened since the fifties. Of course we're getting bored.

Malcolm McLaren, 1988

What I hate about it is there's no evil in it.

Harold Budd on "New Age" music, 1989

I am so much geekier than any of those kids dreaming about me.

Eddie Van Halen

Andrew Lloyd Webber is gobshit. I wouldn't do anything he's associated with.

Roland Gift, rejecting the role of Che Guevara in the movie version of *Evita*, 1989

You know, it's a funny thing about music. The worst thing you can do is *think*. That's the lowest.

Neil Young, 1989

Once upon a time it was enough to know that U2 are crap. But not any more. Now you've got to know *why* they're crap.

Julian Cope, 1983

Makes you feel sad, doesn't it? Like your grandfather died . . . Yeah, it's just too bad it couldn't have been Mick Jagger.

Malcolm McLaren, on the death of Elvis Presley

Fuckin' good riddance to bad rubbish. I don't give a fuckin' shit, and nobody else does either. It's just fun to fake sympathy, that's all they're doin'.

Johnny Rotten, on the death of Elvis Presley

I realized I couldn't give him the kind of adulation he got from his fans, and he *needed* that adulation desperately. Without it he was nothing.

Priscilla Presley, on Elvis

He had to have somebody in bed with him. I don't think sex was even involved lots of the time. He hated to be alone. If there wasn't a girl there, I'd sometimes sleep at the foot of the bed.

Rick Stanley on his stepbrother, Elvis Presley, 1989

"The Kit" went everywhere with Elvis, and I was the guy designated to take care of it. If he went out for a drive, that meant I brought the kit. It had all kinds of uppers—Dexedrine, Black Beauties. Then you've got the Class-A Percodan, Demerol, codeine. There were barbiturates—Tuinal, Seconal, Nembutal, Carbital. Toward the end there was liquid Demerol. Needles. Plus he had money inside the kit—ten grand in a wallet—makeup, a driver's license, and a lot of jewelry.

Rick Stanley, 1989

Elvis Presley—bloated, over the hill, adolescent entertainer—had nothing to do with excellence, just myth.

Marlon Brando, 1979

Prince looks like a dwarf who's been dipped in a bucket of pubic hair.

Boy George, 1986

I apologize, motherfucker, that I am a human being. I fucking apologize. Emotional—you're fucking right. . . . You're full of shit, and I have more fucking balls than you'll ever see. You want to challenge me about emotions, you slimy little man. Fuck you. Fuck you. Don't get peaceful with me. Don't you touch me.

Bill Graham to Steve Gaskin, who claimed that Graham chose "money over love," 1969

Most artists are insecure, I suppose. Insecure overachievers.

Lindsey Buckingham

I'm stockpiling Percodan.

Buster Poindexter, on his investment plans for retirement

When you go on the road, there's nothing to do but do drugs and fuck.

Steven Tyler of Aerosmith

He never contributed a damn thing to much. . . . He was successful, hard to account for.

Bing Crosby, on Elvis Presley

Ray Davies has always been an old man. He writes like an old man who is forever looking back on his life.

Pete Townshend, 1975

There are a lot of guys in the Rock and Roll Hall of Fame who are broke and don't get laid.

Gene Simmons of KISS, on his slim chances for induction into the Rock and Roll Hall of Fame

So what's wrong with cheap, dirty jokes? Fuck you. I never said I was tasteful. I'm *not* tasteful.

Lou Reed, responding to criticism of ethnic slurs in his songs

Once in a while when I turn on the radio in the car, the lyrics I hear are really banal. Toast—when I hear Carole King, I think of toast.

Paul Simon

Rock lyrics are doggerel, maybe.

Dave Marsh

Rock 'n' roll might be summed up as monotony tinged with hysteria.

Vance Packard

Gosh, I just can't understand what would make an intelligent girl like Jessica Hahn debase herself like that.

Julie Brown, on Hahn's role in Sam Kinison's heavy-metal video "Wild Thing"

Ray Charles is nothing but a blind ignorant nigger.

Elvis Costello, 1979

She's totally dominated by a man who never read a book in his life.

Robert Silberstein, Diana Ross's ex-husband, on Berry Gordy

I didn't know nothing about business and business was his thing, so he screwed me. But he screwed me in a teachin' way. So I finally learned how not to get screwed, which is a lesson I'll remember the rest of my life. . . . Yeah, Leonard Chess was like a father to me.

Etta James, on Leonard Chess

I learned to be cheap from Lionel Richie, who is the cheapest person in the world.

Bette Midler

Charlie Watts never could play a solo. And don't believe him when he says he only joined on a temporary basis, ha-ha. It was the only gig he could get.

Mick Jagger, 1978

Brian was a power in the Stones as long as he could pick up any instrument in the studio and get a tune out of it. As soon as he stopped trying and just played rhythm guitar, he was finished.

Andrew Loog Oldham, on Brian Jones

Brian Jones just seemed to deteriorate over the last couple of years of his life. So he wasn't *that* much of a loss, musically.

Bill Wyman, 1969

Brian Jones died about four years after I started wearing black. Strange.

Kyle Byrnes, groupie

I've never been hated by so many people I've never met as in Nebraska in the mid-sixties. Everyone looked at you with a look that could kill. You could tell they just wanted to beat the shit out of you.

Keith Richards

. . . he could never make me feel uncomfortable. Even today, I can squash him with just one word.

Anita Pallenburg, on Mick Jagger

The worst thing of all about being with Mick was this rule he laid down that you must *never* show emotion, in case people realized you weren't cool.

Marianne Faithfull, on Mick Jagger

The worst San Francisco band is better than the best L.A. New Wave group.

Jeff Olener of The Nuns

Jazz has no mystique for me. It reminds me of my dad; it's the institution, the authorities.

Stewart Copeland, 1989

Rod Stewart is a dangerous person as far as I'm concerned, if you're a woman.

Bebe Buell

It really bothers me that a twerp like that can parade around and convince everybody that he's Satan.

Ry Cooder, on Mick Jagger

I think Mick's a joke, with all that fag dancing; I always did.

John Lennon, on Mick Jagger, 1971

He's not unlike Elton John, who represents the token queen—like Liberace used to. He represents the sort of harmless, bourgeois kind of evil that one can accept with a shrug.

David Bowie, on Mick Jagger

I can't hardly sing, you know what I mean? I'm no Tom Jones and I couldn't give a fuck.

Mick Jagger, on himself

I think Mick Jagger would be astounded and amazed if he realized to how many people he is not a sex symbol but a mother image.

David Bowie, on Mick Jagger

Mick Jagger will eventually become the Chuck Berry of the sixties, constantly parodying himself on stage.

Pete Townshend, 1975

He moves like a parody between a majorette girl and Fred Astaire.

Truman Capote, on Mick Jagger

I really just put any old thing on. Not like Mick, with his fabrics and colors. He's like fucking Greta Garbo.

Charlie Watts, on Mick Jagger, 1989

What are Zsa Zsa Gabor and George Plimpton and all those other society freeloaders doing at a birthday party for Mick Jagger? If the Rolling Stones are the newest mind fuck for the Truman Capote crowd, what does that say about the Stones?

Grace Lichtenstein, *New York Times* reporter

I don't even know my own phone number.

Axl Rose

I think Patti Smith is crap. I think she's so awful. . . . She's just full of rubbish. A *poseur* of the worst kind.

Mick Jagger, 1977

What annoys me is that *he* gets to wiggle his bum, and no one slags *him* off. What's so credible about his buttocks compared to mine?

George Michael, on Bruce Springsteen, 1985

George Michael's butt is like another career for him. He works on it.

Julie Brown, 1990

All I could think about her was B.O.— she wouldn't be bad-looking if she would wash up and glue herself together a little better.

Andy Warhol, on Patti Smith

Spandau Ballet! . . . Amateur hour! Stuff like jamming at rehearsals which you'd chuck out and wouldn't consider putting on plastic. To them, that's a *tour de force.*

Johnny Rotten, 1981

You can't drink on an eight-hour flight, pass out, and then go on stage . . . Well, you can, but then you're Spandau Ballet.

Robert Smith of The Cure, 1985

The Smiths are more important than The Police! We're more important than they ever were, or ever will be.

Johnny Marr, 1984

I think The Sex Pistols have copped out. Now they're on the front of *Rolling Stone.* That's a real cop-out.

Mick Jagger

It's a real feeling of deja vu. They puked at the London airport; we pissed in the filling station.

Keith Richards, on The Sex Pistols

Sting was boring and pretentious. Everyone was driven to distraction by his endless speeches on political matters.

Kathleen Turner, 1988

John's just jealous because I'm the brains of the group. I've written all the songs, even from the beginning when I wasn't in the group. They were so useless they had to come to me because they couldn't think of anything by themselves.
Sid Vicious, 1977

This group The Sex Pistols pukes on stage? I don't necessarily like that. That's not showmanship . . . They gotta get themselves an act.
Bo Diddley, 1978

The only way we made it was with a great big old bag of Mexican reds and two gallons of Robitussin HC. Five reds and a slug of HC and you can sleep through anything.
Butch Trucks of The Allman Brothers Band, on touring with eleven people in an Econoline van

. . . she hasn't got a look and she's got a dumpy body and no talent that I can see.
Dave Mustaine of Megadeth, on Tiffany, 1988

. . . people who like smack also like Lou Reed, and that can't be anything in its favor.
Lemmy Motorhead, on why he doesn't do heroin, 1979

He was a great fuck.

**Boy George, on former
bandmate Jon Moss, 1989**

. . . her I.Q. is equivalent to her new bra size . . . [which] must be 32 now. I have nothing positive to say about her. She never taught me anything about film or music or anything worth having a conversation about.

Appolonia, on Vanity, 1989

It will replace nothing, except maybe suicide.

**Cher, on The Velvet
Underground**

Amphetamine doesn't give you peace of mind, but it makes not having it very amusing.

Andy Warhol

Artists like U2 and Bruce Springsteen, who are more directly linked to me, I find very wanting.

Pete Townshend, 1989

. . . I'll wear anything as long as it hasn't been on George Michael's back.

Boy George, 1989

If you wanna sell records, I'm told you gotta make videos. I know they're thought of as an art form, but I don't think they are . . . I've never known what anybody's doing with me. They filmed me from 30 yards away—what are they looking at? When I saw the video all I saw was a shot of me from my mouth to my forehead on the screen. I figure, isn't that something? I'm *paying* for that?

Bob Dylan, 1985

Most videos are pretty much an insult to people's intelligence.

Joe Jackson

Vapid trash intended to sell records.

Harlan Ellison, on music videos

You can take a bunch of young people and you can make them into the Boy Scouts or into Hitler Youth, depending on what you teach them, and MTV's definitely a bad influence.

Ted Turner

Keith was a very positive musician, a very positive performer, but a very negative animal. He needed you for his act—on and off stage.

Peter Townshend, on Keith Moon

Somebody said to me, ''But the Beatles were antimaterialistic.'' That's a huge myth. John and I literally used to sit down and say, ''Now, let's write a swimming pool.''

Paul McCartney, 1990

Jackie would go to bed with anything that was young enough or old enough. If you could pull down your panties and pull up your dress, you could be had by Jackie.

Lee Angel, groupie/stripper, on Jackie Wilson

No, that's The Who.

Ron Wood, when asked if The Rolling Stones had reunited simply to cash in, 1989

Of course we're doing it for the money *as well* . . . we've always done it for the money.

Mick Jagger, 1989

The Who and The Stones are revolting. All they're good for is making money.

Johnny Rotten, 1986

I don't like people like Rod Stewart and Elton John, and I don't like the way they carry on. I get very upset at being identified with that kind of person.

Mick Jagger, 1978

Okay, I confess. I do have this thing about Catholic singing sisters with dark hair who make records for Warner Bros.

Loudon Wainwright III, on his romance with Suzzy Roche of The Roches

He had every social disease I think that's possible. . . . He was infested, and so was his hair. He hadn't taken a bath for months. Or combed his hair. I think it was not so much rock and roll and not so much the road as it is [sic] that nobody was taking care of him. You can always spot a bachelor!

Gail Zappa, on Frank Zappa at the time of their courtship

My weight's a great burden to bear in our quest for commercial success. I don't know why people have such trouble with it. Live, Pere Ubu is simply one of the most amazing things you've ever seen. I think it's well worth having to put up with my size for the privilege of seeing something you'd never, in your wildest dreams, believed you'd love so much. If I was skinny, it wouldn't be Pere Ubu, would it?

Dave Thomas of Pere Ubu, 1989

. . . historically, musicians have felt real hurt if the audience expressed displeasure with their performance. They apologized and tried to make the people love them. We didn't do that. We told the audience to get fucked.

Frank Zappa

It's very easy to presume that I'm not a human being.

Frank Zappa

I think that these are perilous times that we live in, with the influx of singing groups . . . I always have the feeling that that's the *real* invasion of the body-snatchers—the real Martian invasion—they've come here in a guise of folk singers and large singing groups and rock 'n' roll groups, and they're going to get us if we're not careful.

Woody Allen, ca. 1965

I think Townshend's always wanted to be me.

Roger Daltrey, 1975

I enjoyed those shows I did in London at The Rainbow . . . I kept thinking, Frank Zappa fell seventeen feet down into that pit. I hate Frank Zappa, and it made me so happy to think about that.
Lou Reed, 1975

He probably scared the shit out of his mother, too.
Gail Zappa, on Frank Zappa

I thought they called him Omelet 'cause he liked to eat omelets, the way they call a cat Hamhocks who eats hamhocks.
Otis Redding, when corrected on the name of Atlantic Records president Ahmet Ertegun

He's talked himself up his own arse.
Roger Daltrey, on Pete Townshend, 1975

Rock is freedom. Welcome to the Gulag.
Harlan Ellison, 1985

Popular culture is disposable, like Kleenex.
Malcolm McLaren, 1988

I don't really give a fuck anymore about what anyone thinks of me.
Paul Weller, 1985

I have a toilet mentality—I don't give a shit what people know about me.
Linda Thompson, 1985

Even stars get tired of talking about themselves. Some of them can talk intelligently, but a lot of them can't even hold a decent conversation. They know nothing but rock, and not a lot about that. It makes it difficult to get a decent interview. A lot of times, you'll be lucky to get more than muttering and stuttering.
Bill Graham

Ass-deep in apocryphal anecdotes, we slough our way through the debris of society toward a dubious future in which, one day, the U.S. Postal Service will issue a Barry Manilow stamp in "Great Americans" series.
Harlan Ellison, 1985

Rock and roll has become respectable. What a bummer.
Ray Davies, 1990

*[Don't let the bastards get you down].

Index